CH00241306

IN THE

WORDS OF...

Copyright Ken Ross

IN THE WORDS OF...

By Ken Ross

Books by this author:

Brainbox
Tables Are Fun
Spooky Towers
The Spy With The Missing Brain
Joke File
Animal Crackers
Yucky Chuckles
School Screamers
Monster Giggles
Fantasy Football
On Your Marks
Master Class: Play Acting
St. Dodgers' School Yearbook
Halloween
Pirate
Code Busters
Dracula
Alien
Werewolf
Frankenstein
Witch
Top Secret
Spy File
Essential School Fun File
Private Detective
Skeleton
Looking For Twiggy

INTRODUCTION

Life is a game, and the object of the game is to live according to our own beliefs whilst adhering to the rules of the society in which we reside. Unfortunately for most of us, the burdens of existence determine how we actually proceed on life's path. The time devoted to work, the necessity of serving our responsibilities, and the unforeseeable twists of fate take their toll and we are left living a semi-satisfactory life within the restrictions of what is possible. We should have no grumbles with this system, for if the determination and fortitude we show is strong, there are ways of exceeding the expectations perhaps our parents had for us, and we may discover prospects that more suit our individually tailored requirements of what is ideal. The game of life is fun, the rewards are self-satisfying, and so we need to do all we can to acquire the wisdom that shall assist us in reaching our goals.

Life's basic rules are quickly learned. By four years old we are conscious of the position we hold in the scheme of things. We know our governors, the rank held among siblings and relatives, the vague merits of our dwelling place, and we are aware of the prevailing conditions in our close social area. We fit in position for as yet in the process of development nothing has given us the clue that our position is changeable or that one day in the future the seeds of dissatisfaction may be sown. A child at four years old remains in the early fascination stage where a majority of life's nuances is a mystery. As yet aphorisms or words of wisdom appear as gentle rebukes from a parent.

No sooner than we have gone to school does the huge realization appear that life is about learning lessons. The first mistakes we make are mighty ones – so easily rectified but so memorable in experience. That stone is harder and more brutal than skin has to be learned. That gravity will bring us to earth, that knowledge has to be grasped, that emotions steer us, that we are tip-toeing though our mortality, yes, all have to be learned. We become gluttonous and refine what we do and what we think by the insatiable hunger for living that drives us. However many lessons we learn, and come to understand their significances, we know there is an endless ocean of lessons yet to be encountered. By early adulthood we can look both backward and forward; we can see ourselves raw in childhood and hope for wisdom in the future.

Morality and the sense of what is right and wrong are much clearer to the young adult than to the four year old child. Perhaps we are not aware but we will be blurting the same truths repeatedly and these truths will be the backbone of our social existence. All the habits that make us what we are will be performed under the constraints of our morality. We will exhibit that which is us to all that is within our social circles as a sign that we are at one with everything around us. Seldom will we deviate from the personal traits that define us, and we will expect others to recognize us by the very things by which we define ourselves. Through all of our experience the chisel that has been sculpting our character has been held in the hand of the word. The word, the enormous influence of language, has been secretly shaping us from the occasion our first word was uttered. What we believe is a collection of words. We think in words and communicate in words. We are attracted by the word and repelled by the word. The words we speak are the badge of our mind.

Fortunate human beings pass through many decades, and the more decades we encounter the greater number of opportunities arise for refining and toning our wisdom. Past experience always warns us that what we think today is susceptible to the new information of tomorrow. Even long held opinions and beliefs are shot to pieces by startling revelations. Our pool of wisdom is forever ebbing and flowing and experience tells us that we should never cease catching the raindrops or be at all surprised if our pool is inundated by waters from the flood. Many ideas we have held dear change in complexion throughout adulthood. If we are receptive to challenges to our ideas we may see retrospectively that the challenges were merited. At the end of every decade of life we should be able to congratulate ourselves on further progress on the road to wisdom. Our peers stand ready to guide us: they are friends whose gifts have no cost.

All through life the ideas of what we wish for ourselves gain clarity. We come to know what we don't wish for and have experiences of things that we never want to be repeated. Our priorities alter, and as the potential of years remaining decreases we realize that priorities play a significant part in the way in which we organize our lives. By utilizing that which we have learned we find methods of serving our major priorities and reasonably become a little selfish with our time. Increasingly the statement 'we have one life' rings in the mind. It is senseless to spend time doing what is uncomfortable if there exists opportunity to take comfort. Our learning helps us manipulate circumstance to get what we want. We are wise to our own needs and we have a right to demand that our time is given to our whims or our comforts. Oh yes, wisdom is enlightening but it is also a powerful ally.

Life is our own: it is our most precious asset. There is no denying that we have some kind of sense of duty to society, to our country, to our family, to those who depend on us, but as harshly as it may sound we have a greater sense of duty to the self, and it is a betrayal of the self if we forfeit that duty and die unfulfilled in our dreams. The discovery of our dreams is the first step in fulfilling them. The remaining steps are all related to the knowledge gathering process, the acquisition of wisdom, and in the use of expediency. Wily old folks can teach youth a thing or two about the latter.

What matters most is what we want most. The game of life is about collecting the skills necessary in order to create a life that is both fulfilling and comfortable. A world brimful of contented souls should provide a harmonious co-existence, although it can be said that contentedness is an enemy of progress.

Being a small child in the 1950's was an introduction to sayings like 'children should be seen and not heard' and 'no good will come out of it'. There was also the 'don't answer adults back', which seemed a rather stupid statement after a question had been asked. At some point in life a recalcitrant child is bound to respond to these idiocies with words of his own. The statements that are collected in this book are thoughts I have had about life. Hopefully they will give rise to thoughts in the minds of readers. Some statements will not necessarily find agreement, but if they provoke discussion or challenge, then that it fine.

IN THE WORDS OF...

Long ago, when man lived in his cave with wench and offspring, the world was a dangerous place. Not only did Ugg the caveman exist without modern conveniences, but he was probably bereft of a coherent language. Ugg doubtless hunted from first light to sunset. After he'd dragged home a heavy buffalo calf for Mrs Ugg to disembowel and for her to later cook over a twig-fuelled fire, he'd stretch his hairy limbs and settle down on a bed of smelly grass, and nod off.

Of course, it was cold in the cave. Ugg seldom, if ever, fell into a deep sleep. The biting wind often chilled him as it found the gaps in his loin cloth, and the noises from outside the cave spoke to him of creatures on the move and of meat eaters sensing blood. Ugg kept his heavy club close by as danger was ever present.

One clear, cold night Ugg was disturbed by a scraping sound outside the entrance to his cave. One eye opened quickly. Ugg noticed Baby Ugg was absent from her bedding spot. Immediately he was on his feet with club in hand and he raced to the cave's entrance. The silver moon lit the sky and cast pools of light on the uneven terrain. His daughter was scratching a large rock with a hand-sized stone in her hand. Ugg was relieved, then...

Horror struck him as a bear strode from trees not two man's lengths from Baby Ugg.

A mighty roar blasted from Ugg's mouth as with raised club he charged the bear and snatched the girl in his free arm. The bear began to lunge forward, but altered its track and retreated from the fearless caveman. Ugg roared a second time, and the bear was gone.

Inside the cave Mrs Ugg embraced her daughter. Ugg stood over them both. He grunted a stream of soft noises, which translated into modern language as 'The child who leaves the cave shall become food for the bear'.

From Ugg's time to the present, words of wisdom have been in existence: these words guide us and they warn us. Wise words are passed down through the generations as precious tools of our inheritance. There has been many benefactors over the ages, and each one of them added to the library of human knowledge. It is my hope that one or two of my written thoughts will remain in the collection long after I have gone.

1. Doubt and uncertainty fuel the search for knowledge.

2. A butterfly's frailty is not apparent to a tiny insect.

3. An open gate troubles only the fence builder.

4. Birds fly faster when a man has both feet on the ground.

5. Evolution matches the changes of its environment.

6. Health is the last worry of the healthy.

7. Give a child happy memories and he will become a collector.

8. A tree, unlike a human, will always seek the light.

9. Regret is negative: correction is positive.

10. Religion is solace for those who can't face extinction.

11. Truth stands in our path no matter which way we flee.

12. There can be no comfort without hardship.

13. Nothing is more precious than the gift of time.

14. Advice given freely is always worth careful

    consideration.

15. Parenthood is something once gotten in to is never

    gotten out of.

16. Love is the burden of our associations.

17. Punctuality is a clue to trustworthiness.

18. Those who lick their lips are seeking prey.

19. A mother who curses her sons shall feel the hurt of

    their neglect.

20. The want of money for money's sake comes from he

    who has a hollow heart.

21. Those whose fascination never wanes are blessed

    with the spirit of childhood.

22. People who listen hear more than people who talk.

23. Toothache is the dimmest warning of our mortality.

24. Diets are for those who constantly think about food.

25. Differences of opinion should be shared, not

    sharpened.

26. The use of the words I, me, myself, betrays a lack of

    recognition that there are other people in the world.

27. Memory is the selective recall of the past.

28. Admit nothing and the onus of proof is on the

    accuser.

29. A lame duck never swims straight.

30. Even the world's strongest man can never lift

    himself without assistance.

31. The view through a window is only a partial view of

    reality.

32. The best response to a lie is no response.

33. A child without manners becomes an adult with questionable morality.

34. Answer a child's questions and one day he will reward you with answers to your own questions.

35. A man fails to find a button in a drawer but sees danger on the horizon.

36. Only humans own clocks.

37. War is the interruption between peace talks.

38. Marooned on a desert island, no man would wear a shirt and tie.

39. One step from disaster still affords an escape route.

40. It is not questions which are avoided – it is answers.

41. History is the debris of man's existence.

42. Children see what their eyes see: adults see what they think their minds have seen.

43. Suspicion is the result of being once right in a thousand assumptions.

44. Genius is the art of simplification.

45. The high tower of indifference provides protection against that which is emotionally destructive.

46. A fair society is one which treats people how they deserve to be treated.

47. A contented man harbors no wishes.

48. Many adults forget they have been children, and many children forget this kind of adults.

49. Luck is the result of creating possibilities and he who creates most will receive the most luck.

50. Life is a continuous replay of old habits.

51. Tea drinkers are predictable, wine drinkers sociable, and water drinkers impressionable.

52. Truthfulness is the defense of the weak and the weapon of the wise.

53. Going bald is much worse than being bald.

54. A man without a pen has no thought worth writing.

55. Poverty is not a trap, it is a starting point.

56. The rich man and the poor man find equality beneath their tombstones.

57. Jewelry soothes those who are not entirely comfortable in their own skin.

58. Women notice women.

59. There are no addicts in a crisis.

60. In a democracy everything finds disagreement.

61. The most readable language is emotion.

62. Those who raise their hands high to applaud wish to be seen. Those who hands are lower wish their applause to be heard.

63. Beyond the final page lies only the cover.

64. Offer women sympathy, not solutions.

65. We talk about the weather when no serious desire to communicate exists.

66. No amount of forgiveness can wipe away a stained memory

67. No-one is famous in the darkness and the silence.

68. The distance to yesterday is immeasurable.

69. Rather than borrow, deny yourself the pleasure of getting into debt.

70. Spectators gain pleasure from the achievements of others.

71. A cheat can always be trusted to cheat.

72. A government's priority should be the welfare of

   law-abiding, tax-paying citizens.

73. A country's prospects depend on the education of its

   children.

74. A party politician has no voice of his own.

75. The right to bear children comes with responsibility.

76. All people possess talents; however the talent of

   some is more apparent than the talent of others.

77. Beware a pair of laughing lips beneath a pair of eyes

   that dip.

78. A firm handshake impresses only a firm hand-

   shaker.

79. A bald head carries no raindrops.

80. Each generation refines the rules of life to incur the chagrin of older generations.

81. Sheep and cows don't ask questions.

82. A changing horizon means you are on the move.

83. Nothing brings you down to earth like gravity.

84. The desire for equality is to recognize that we are unequal.

85. A man comes home to his wife and goes to the home of his mistress.

86. Parents wish to feel comfort from their daughters and to feel proud of their sons.

87. A woman will always submit when she is proved right.

88. Long-legged people don't always take things in their stride.

89. Exams are for those with replicated learning.

90. The ownership of an ashtray is no proof of a smoker.

91. Beyond reasonable doubt is not certainty.

92. They are those who you are not.

93. A parent's description of a child is more accurate than a child's description of its parent.

94. A woman who speaks too much is seldom heard.

95. Your first century begins with wonderment, and so does your second.

96. Mollycoddled boys make lazy husbands.

97. The truth is often an insult which most people don't wish to receive.

98. A gardener has no arguments with his flowers.

99. Words are the swords and shields of a non-violent society.

100. Those who sit in circles do not take sides.

101. There can be no expansion of an infinite universe; there can be only gravitational fluxes.

102. The habitually cold-natured can hardly expect to receive kind remarks said to others.

103. To be wise after the event necessitates an eventful life.

104. A man walks as fast as his mind tells him to.

105. Beauty is no measure of a good mother.

106. Food intake equals energy minus exercise.

107. Knowledge earns no-one rights of social superiority.

108. When responses overweigh the enquirer the human is stultified.

109. Four quarters can still have three quarters missing.

110. Trust not a child to wander in water.

111. The young who scoff at the old will one day, if they

are fortunate, feel retribution.

112. No is the best excuse of all.

113. Criticism should be given only on request.

114. A man who begs for favors is an unfavorable

wretch.

115. Guilt is exposed by the over-interested.

116. The intelligent underestimate those with a higher

intelligence.

117. He who refutes an answer desires a different one.

118. Speak only of hard times with those who shared

them.

119. Be astounded by your own genius – few others will

be.

120. Nothing ages man more than the age of his woman.

121. Hands held out in greed deprive those hands held

out in necessity.

122. Life is no more than a film in which the self appears

only in reflections.

123. Habits are the backbone of existence.

124. Experience reduces complication to ease.

125. Where the eyes rest the brain finds gentle

amusement.

126. Ideas are simply a matter of juxtaposing words.

127. To create in a rush is better than to labor to create.

128. Images of art stay truer in the mind than images of

reality.

129. Grief doesn't kill: loneliness does.

130. Hearts only remember a comfortable embrace.

131. Charity, once repeated, never feels like a kind endeavor.

132. Spoken hopes are dashed once we share them with enemies.

133. Words heard that are not said resound within a worried head.

134. Speak ill of the dead and the living will speak ill of you.

135. Truth is given once whilst lies are repeated.

136. An employer will reduce payment for a job not fully complete whilst an unwise employee will do more work than for that he is paid.

137. Decisions define where we have been and they also determine our destiny.

138. Morality is the rulebook which governs our actions.

139. All people deserve human rights save those who abuse their rights to humanity.

140. It is only the inadequate who show jealousy of possessions.

141. Satiated desires lead to habits.

142. Judge others from your perspective and they are entitled to judge you from theirs.

143. Seeing the positive brings hope; seeing the negative brings despair.

144. A wise word is better than a prison sentence.

145. Nothing shakes belief like a personal tragedy.

146. The dullest people are those who live in small worlds.

147. Blood is thickest in a crisis.

148. A pointing finger carries no bullets.

149. Happy children make no demands.

150. The gloom of existence evaporates in the glee of

   laughter.

151. Pain free poverty is preferable to painful wealth.

152. A panicking parent is no comfort to an injured child.

153. Open hands hold no secrets.

154. He who loves not spring shall never laugh or smile

   or sing.

155. Only the determined walk against the wind.

156. Impossibilities are the stepping stones of progress.

157. Friendship comes with the cost of time.

158. Lost loves never age in dreams.

159. A man feels smaller without his shoes on.

160. Organized minds never lose their keys.

161. When the ball rolls from the child's hand the child
has learned the laws of force and motion.

162. Familiar things are viewed with less clarity than new
things.

163. To desire the unobtainable is a wasted act of desire.

164. Keen eyes never recount obviously simple solutions.

165. It is a bad gambler who only remembers his
successes.

166. Good men make predictable husbands.

167. Fiction is always believable.

168. A child who wants for nothing will always desire
more.

169. Always focus on the whole for a segment is
invariably misleading.

170. The weak only perish when the strong lack compassion.

171. Unwarranted description is the first act of prejudice.

172. Participate because you want to, not because you think you must.

173. When the left hand moves chaotically, the right hand needs watching.

174. The joy of outliving contemporaries is balanced by the sadness of their demises.

175. Little is expected of younger siblings that older ones have not accomplished.

176. Give a man a job if he is grateful of the chance of employment.

177. Kind deeds beg no reward.

178. A promise is a commitment the conscience can

struggle to fulfill.

179. The poor never pray for praise.

180. The youngest child shall reap all the benefits of its

parents' experience.

181. The banging head will crack before the brick wall.

182. Weaken your enemy with kind words.

183. A man tells of where he is going and a woman says

where she is now.

184. The primary strategy of a winner is to determine

how not to lose.

185. The neck shrinks as the liar thinks.

186. Tell no more than is asked of you, then there is

always more to tell.

187. He who finishes first is often best but sometimes worst.

188. Those who are lost know from where they came.

189. One apple will provide enough apples for a lifetime.

190. Believe not what society tells you, but what you have learned from society.

191. You can't swim uphill.

192. The qualities of objectivity and foresightedness make for a good leader.

193. Mathematics is the single perfection.

194. Belief has no sensible beginning but always has a sensible end.

195. Smells and sounds are the stringed balloons of memories.

196. In times of uncertainty you can be sure of where

you are.

197. Gossip is an explosion of reality.

198. A woman has begun her training by the age of four.

199. Desperation is the lax father of justification.

200. The imagination of childhood survives only in the

rarest adults.

201. The economic fortunes of a country fluctuate

according to the moods of optimism or pessimism in

the minds of the country's working people.

202. Never risk stability for that which is uncertain.

203. The legacy of the majority is children.

204. A democracy falters when the ruling party is

incompetent or corrupt and the opposition parties

offer no substantive hope of amelioration.

205. An electoral vote should be earned by having

contributed to that which the voter hopes to elect.

206. A young woman delights an old man's eye.

207. A man's downfall is to live with a cake-baker.

208. Life's priority is to grow old.

209. All things change save your favorite songs.

210. A constant talker hates to be sidelined.

211. The whole world is home for the astronaut.

212. A deep thinker doesn't always agree with his

thoughts.

213. Both a country and a family are united by a tragedy.

214. A sport that is unfairly played is no more than a

spectacle of farce.

215. Memories contained in the mind hold greater detail

than our conscious mind usually recounts.

216. Without religious tolerance there can be no religious freedom.

217. A human is but a cake-mix of its ancestors' genes.

218. No economist could balance the books of the impecunious.

219. The proof of existence is in the clarity of non-existence.

220. A wise man may listen to a fool but he will never offer him advice.

221. Is it not right to fight for your homeland?

222. Ramifications of problems are not problems: the problem is the problem.

223. A society that teaches its children untruths shall at some later date pay the price.

224. What we say in anger, we repent in leisure.

225. Don't blame the instrument for what it may deliver.

226. Quiet words are the ones heard loudest.

227. Those who prepare for the future shall inherit a life of comfort.

228. Good manners make no enemies.

229. The greatest teachers light the spark of learning in their pupils.

230. You are always a stranger in new clothes.

231. Evidence speaks louder than speculation.

232. Originality is the total dilution of influences.

233. There is no compromise in genius.

234. Treat every failure as an act of correction.

235. The sweetest sadness is that which reminds us of our youth.

236. Question everything and the path to cynicism will

widen.

237. A politician saves his own neck first.

238. A conformist attitude is a prerequisite of

employment in uniform.

239. A worker will oblige whilst a thinker argues.

240. There is no such thing as a tiny prejudice.

241. Complication is no barrier to a child filled with

enthusiasm.

242. Speak of one's past with measured interest but

speak of one's future with hope.

243. A limited fund is a feeble excuse for not trying to

fulfill an ambition.

244. Cried tears are to some mere confectionery and to

others stone boulders.

245. Bad habits are also recognized by those who have

acquired them.

246. At birth no child has a religion.

247. It is wrong to undervalue a bricklayer before or

after an earthquake.

248. Nature's response to mankind is to show him his

frailties.

249. Submission is expediency in the face of disaster.

250. Wise words resound on others' tongues.

251. A screaming baby arouses what a crying baby does

not.

252. Lies are mere pins and the truth is a spear.

253. Benevolence should pull a man to his feet then

allow him to walk unaided.

254. Education is a gift from older generations, not a product for which our young should pay.

255. Those who don't understand can't explain.

256. An umbrella is no use in a flood.

257. The right of a child to its parents is equal to the rights of its parents to the child.

258. In the young a cry for forgiveness is disguised as a cry for help.

259. The market value of a property is of no consequence to those who are staying put.

260. Study mediocrity and that will be the limit of your ambition.

261. Fame only extends to those who are interested.

262. Statistics do not prevent men from setting precedents.

263. A book is only as good as the mind it entertains.

264. The fewer burdens imposed on an economy, the more buoyant it becomes.

265. Infatuation is a term used by adults to describe unapproved youthful love.

266. As children we take flight, and as teenagers we soar to the heavens; for the remainder of our lives we glide back down to earth.

267. Laws differ from country to country, and therefore so too the definition of a criminal.

268. To think that which has never been thought one must possess a capacious mind and a sieve the size of an atom.

269. It is not how proficiently you sing but how uniquely original your voice resounds.

270. Those who seek to impress do not know the true measure of their talent, or lack of it.

271. The proudest moments of the selfless are given by other people's kindnesses.

272. The imagination should not be doomed to hibernation by the constraints of adulthood.

273. You are what you have been longest.

274. Capitalism flourishes when everyone, to some degree, is a capitalist.

275. When we have less, still we have more than some.

276. A global economy doesn't always favor those who believe it will favor them.

277. The more comfortable a society becomes the greater its imperfections will be magnified.

278. The danger of punishment is recalcitrance: the

merit of correction is conformity.

279. To give more than is needed is a recipe for

expectation.

280. Be a judge with evidence or be one of the scurrilous

who condemn the innocent.

281. Three children are three times more problematic

than two children.

282. A government with five years tenure of office

doesn't have a fifty year outlook.

283. Malicious thoughts are destructive only to the self.

284. The practice of life is a continuous assumption.

285. Sleep is the page we turn before the next chapter.

286. Minds select information they need to fortify what

their mouth have already uttered.

287. Shady characters seldom appear otherwise.

288. It is easier to disappoint than to satisfy.

289. When talent is limited and opportunities are rare, don't easily condemn a man who has dealt with the devil.

290. Those who expect higher morality than that which we can deliver weigh heavy on the conscience.

291. True compassion comes from those whose love has no cost.

292. Mature laughter is an appreciative smile.

293. The city dweller finds familiarity in a foreign city but is bewildered by the countryside of his homeland.

294. We are merely transport for our genes.

295. Don't spend the future paying for the past.

296. Any fool can be wise retrospectively.

297. No age reaches the moral perfections of ages to

come.

298. Gossip and truth come alike to the busybody.

299. A child often gives the answer which the adult

wishes to hear.

300. When horrendous sins of a hitherto perceived good

man are revealed, public opinion paints him a bad

man: he is both a good man and a bad man, and has

always been thus.

301. Laws which have served a society well for

generations should not be repealed due to a rare

circumstance of events.

302. Ask not what you can give the less fortunate; ask

the less fortunate what they require.

303. A good book tells you what you don't know.

304. Fluency is the art of everything.

305. Only the middle classes can prosper or fail.

306. Political divisions are healable: religious divisions are not.

307. A society may imprison a man's body but it can't imprison his mind.

308. Life after death is only thought credible by the living.

309. A society is selective in its choice of past crimes which should be solved.

310. Each generation's knowledge and beliefs are sifted through the minds of its children, and after revision a fresh age of enlightenment commences.

311. The more man denies other species to co-exist on earth, the greater the threat of his closest competitors, the rodents.

312. The inhabitation of a second planet would bring to mankind the stark realization that human life on earth must be sustainable.

313. Aspirations are more easily achieved when the number of aspirants is limited.

314. The good always refute the truths uttered by the wicked.

315. A man with a spear can't outrun an antelope, but his endurance as a runner can tire the beast, and thus he will get his dinner.

316. Good fortune should never be expected, only welcomed when it arrives.

317. When you're trust is betrayed, then you have made

a bad judgment of character,

318. The fearful live behind locked doors,

319. Celibacy is like never having gone abroad.

320. Don't share your interests with the disinterested.

321. Never respect those who keep you waiting for they

don't respect you.

322. You never know when you've lived half your life.

323. To place a stick in a tiny stream high in the

mountains, and to persuade it by gentle

encouragement and guidance to join the source of

the river, and then to repeat this care and attention

until the stick finds the river mouth and meets the

freedom of the ocean, is the precise nature of

parenthood.

324. Flattery is effective on those who least anticipate its arrival.

325. Those who easily revise their opinions seldom blame themselves for the opinions they once held.

326. An act of charity by a wicked man is still an act of charity.

327. Money is the modern god.

328. A child learns quicker about life than a parent does about children.

329. Suffering has no interludes.

330. Corruption is the crime of the ruling classes.

331. Freedom rises meekly from the vast body of sacrifice.

332. No amount of learning can teach a man to think.

333. A good critic need not possess the skills to surpass that he criticizes, however he must be able to identify the skills which are necessary for higher achievement.

334. Never try to fool those who have walked a path before you.

335. A river's water always falls upstream.

336. Individuality is our rarest quality and the one which should illuminate our existence.

337. Those who cry wolf shall be slaughtered by lambs.

338. Contentment is the art of finding gentle amusement.

339. A man sees the alphabet and a woman sees its letters.

340. Only the dubious would wish both to solve a

mystery and to keep a secret.

341. Erasing the memory of a person's existence is a

betrayal of your own insecurity.

342. Preparing for old age is both sensible and

optimistic.

343. Rules and regulations are impediments to progress.

344. Possessions are the baggage of the ego.

345. Freedom of speech applies only to the single voice

in the wilderness.

346. If politicians were shopkeepers their empty

premises would have fine window displays.

347. Those who live on the glory of past achievements

have no more to offer.

348. Each home should be governed as an independent state, and each state should be governed as an independent home.

349. It is the prerogative of all people to either stagnate or prosper.

350. The morality of one age is the immorality of another.

351. The public's memory has the lifespan of a headline.

352. The rich will exploit the loyalty of the poor.

353. A brute given power will inflict brutality on his underlings.

354. The young should be forgiven a surplice of enthusiasm.

355. The wealthy old are master puppeteers of those with greedy hopes of inheritance.

.

356. A keen eye never blinks when its notices one who

strays from a lifetime's habits.

357. Acts borne from a sense of duty prevent the

emergence of guilty feelings.

358. No scene can be viewed as it was decades earlier

for time changes it and our perception of it changes

more.

359. We hang our memories on the fictional places of

reality.

360. The wrongs of the world melt in the daily struggle

for survival.

361. A dearth of pity is a characteristic of the

unintelligent.

362. The oldest allegiances bear the greatest evidence of

their justification.

363. The question why has the simplest answer which is

not satisfactorily received by the majority.

364. Small lessons in life, accumulatively, bring about

great wisdom.

365. Receive compliments with a thank you and

criticisms with gratitude.

366. Never heap praise on those who tomorrow you may

condemn.

367. In the desert water is worth more than gold.

368. The witch hunters will always find a witch to

persecute.

369. Youth flounders in our late twenties, by thirty two it

is dead, and a new wave of philosophical thinking

laps in the mind.

370. Look on your past as the intriguing story which led you to today.

371. An unloved child is fated to become an adult unable to express love.

372. Happiness reigns when all routes lead home.

373. Only a parent can empathize with another parent about their children.

374. Condescension is an assumption of inferiority.

375. The index finger should never support the lower lip in honest speech.

376. When the masses rise up the minorities take cover.

377. Fortune can only be evaluated from a standpoint of personal safety, for without safety there are no certain prospects.

378. Urgent situations require priority of thought.

379. When nature flexes its muscle man must show his

humility.

380. There is no greater reminder of suffering than when

the self becomes a sufferer.

381. View small pleasures as treasures and life will never

be found wanting.

382. Age is no barrier to a youthful mind.

383. Life's defining moment comes when first meeting

astonishment.

384. A philosophical nature is one which considers all

things but expects nothing in particular.

385. Solutions are easier to identify than to implement.

386. We pass the first and second decades of life

witnessing what we believe to be the greatest

human achievements; the remainder of life, in part,

is devoted to defending these views.

387. Morally, discrimination is unjustifiable: logically, an

act of discrimination occurs when we discriminate

against those who have been discriminatory.

388. We are foreigners once we stray from our

birthplace.

389. A woman's handbag contains that which she alone

knows she needs.

390. A charitable donation should not be an act of

conscience but a response to pity we feel for victims

supported by the charity.

391. The worst judges of an event are those who hold

preconceived ideas about its outcome.

392. Handle misfortune philosophically rather than allow

it to result in paranoia.

393. Ignorant age will not bow to wise youth.

394. To listen and observe reaps the best yield.

395. A caring child will not stray far from its parents'

nest.

396. Do not believe in the illusion of what is important;

believe what experience tells you is of note.

397. Food is merely fuel, however sumptuously it is

presented.

398. Pleasant reflection is the poor companion of

dreams and hopes.

399. The drafts of today are tomorrow's pages.

400. When presentation is everything, substance is

nothing.

401. To share one's money is generosity but to share one's time is true benevolence.

402. A written thought is evidence of a brain that functions.

403. No elected leader's policies have mattered more than his personality.

404. The abuse of a position of authority demands an immediate and permanent downfall.

405. Silence and stillness brings an active child to rest.

406. Those who stand by the exit are not staying.

407. You will only see couples half as much if you only like one of them.

408. An overbearing father frees his sons only on his demise.

409. The personal fear of the shame of losing is the chief asset of the winner.

410. Creative minds are not interested in personal glory, only in the glory of creation.

411. A mother's sons are always a mystery to her.

412. The darkest days are those riddled with uncertainty.

413. Judge a man not by his dress but by the manner in which he appears in it.

414. Speak a greeting, kiss a goodbye.

415. A wild wind stirs the wildness in a child.

416. Knowledge enlightens, nature refreshes – only stars shine.

417. Life engages free thinkers in thoughtfulness.

418. The mysteries of existence are solved with death.

419. Anniversaries are spasmodic remembrances.

420. The object of a man's desire never ages.

421. Fulfillment seldom matches the desire.

422. Neither man nor fish dwell on the beach.

423. It is unwise to welcome what we wish to hear

without questioning the voice that speaks.

424. Where there is opportunity for abuse, there will be

abuse.

425. Inflation cripples the poor and causes the middle

classes to scream.

426. When the last child flees the nest the parents are

left with the sobering reality of each other.

427. Melancholy sings loudest when witnessing the

physical toils which the self in younger days was able

to undertake.

428. Copied behavior comes from inferior minds.

429. Modern art is a triumph of thought over artistry.

430. The truth of our experience is the measure by which

all other truths should be judged.

431. It is imperative to identify wisdom whatever its

source, for wisdom arrives both from the

unexpected deliverer and from the sage who has

carried it before.

432. It is the drips of pleasure bad habits provide that

keep followers attracted to bad habits.

433. Weight loss occurs when stood on a set of scales

with eyes fixed on the dial, and waiting.

434. A mistake is an error of judgment; a crime is a

judgment of error.

435. The value of an object is estimable; its sentimental

value is not.

436. Simple rules are the most obeyed.

437. The complication of anything leads to its

malfunction.

438. Familiar noises are least heard.

439. All things can go without food except fire.

440. Compromise is no-one's ideal.

441. There is no such thing as destiny even though it is

the place we all eventually arrive.

442. In a democracy a majority may vote for its downfall.

443. He who tells the same stories should expect an

increasingly disinterested response.

444. Respect may merit admiration, never adoration.

445. A threatened child is doomed to a fearful

adulthood.

446. Moods are states of mind and can be altered quickly by changes of circumstance or location.

447. Emotions in dreams are re-tasted from our life experiences of them.

448. All thoughts are vulnerable to destruction by new thoughts.

449. Successive steps make giant strides.

450. Wealth looks wealth in the eye and taps poverty on the head.

451. Beauty has no comparison and is only revealed amidst ordinariness.

452. Emotion has no defense, only a ceaseless susceptibility to struggle.

453. Boys feign weaknesses to gain their mother's protection.

454. Those who perpetuate historical lies deserve the shame of ignominy.

455. Words are the means the dead use to talk to the living.

456. There is no such entity as still water to those who live in the rapids.

457. Relationships are both founded and sustained by a mutual agreement of time-sharing.

458. Longevity is the result of comfortable living rather than the product of modern medicine.

459. The rightfulness of possession is a clearer determinate than the cost of possession.

460. Each man's delights are a source of mystery to others.

461. Fossils are the ultimate realization of ambitions.

462. Public officials must face scrutiny if we are to place trust in their actions.

463. Those whom a government taxes fairly can never feel fairness has been applied if the system of taxation is not fully inclusive of all citizens and all corporations.

464. Those who fail to succeed by the prevailing rules will always seek to change them.

465. When attitudes change, those with attitude have been stirred.

466. The mean have never embraced the joy of giving.

467. A crowd of helpers will always find recruits.

468. No man dances for his dinner when there is free food.

469. History at its best is the testimony of eye-witnesses; at its worst it is the fantastical musings of scholars.

470. Empty heads talk about their jobs.

471. It is better to live in a society where riches are divided unfairly according to social status than to live where happiness is afforded only to the upper classes.

472. Minor complaints occur in every human but it is only when they are classified and named as illnesses that they become major issues.

473. A present should be something the recipient would appreciate rather than something you have the desire to give.

474. The deserted child will always have a reason to look backwards.

475. A good meal is different for the fox and the chicken.

476. A dysfunctional army can never be permanently

suppressed by an army that is organized and

regimented.

477. There is no glory in doing what is right.

478. The loss of all possessions results in either

nakedness or freedom.

479. Normality is what we are used to: strangeness is

what we are not used to yet.

480. Those who are most resistant to change are the

elderly who have witnessed most changes.

481. Take away a person's habits and you take away a

person's identity.

482. Minds that daily find occupation will feel daily

satisfaction.

483. A huge majority of suspicions is wrong but we

remember the odd occasions when a suspicion is

founded.

484. Debt is an anchor to the ship of progress.

485. A parent may speak words of thanks to kind, adult

children but the pride felt is much greater.

486. By accepting the new we broaden our outlook and

suspend our inflexibility.

487. Art that needs explanation is fabricated.

488. Those who overreact speak louder of their own

failings than of that which has caused the reaction.

489. To severely admonish errors does not encourage

their comfortable correction.

490. One man's view of bravery is another man's act of

necessity.

491. Maturity has set in when you become mindful of

your parents' ages.

492. Within the mind fantasy and reality are one.

493. A winner does not defeat opponents, he lives up to

his self expectations.

494. Queues are recreational facilities for those who

enjoy waiting.

495. The self-reliant are least susceptible to

disappointment.

496. In our third decade of life the spirit of childhood and

the noble aspiration of youth take severe beatings

from our new roles as partner, provider,

housekeeper and parent.

497. We change temporarily but we can never stray too

far from the character with which we were born.

498. Life's past loves never age.

499. The magic of dreams is that all time can exist

simultaneously.

500. The moment of achievement is merely a speck at

the end of a long path of struggle.

501. To venture beyond an intended stopping point

shows interest remains strong.

502. A gift should never cost more than its recipient is

able to afford.

503. The optimist sees growth; the pessimist see

stagnation and decline; the realist gets on with his

work.

504. Intelligence recognizes when it is wrong.

505. It is easier to change how you look that to change

your outlook.

506. The truth is easier to recognize than the lie.

507. Ask others to do only what you are not capable of,

but which you would do if you were capable of

doing.

508. A thought may be abstract but when translated to

words it gains meaningfulness.

509. To people who dress for the occasion the occasion

is never enough.

510. A fundamental rule of society is to be clothed in

public and it is fair to assume that those who adhere

to this basic rule are sane.

511. When the abuses and malfunctions of a society's

conditions are tolerated they will become more

frequent.

512. Shared grief is consolation, but preventing

unnecessary grief is humanness.

513. Laughter is only infectious on the right faces.

514. Voluntary helpers are not always what they seem.

515. Persistency speaks loudest in a crowd of triers.

516. Give a child a feeling of self-worth and it has armor

for life.

517. Most goods are not wanted by an individual but all

goods are wanted by somebody.

518. All conditions and circumstances of life are normal

until they are changed.

519. The nuances of perspective dance to changes of

thought and physical positioning.

520. All are equal in darkness except the sighted

amongst the blind.

521. Youth laughs at aches and pains whilst age fights a

constant duel with them.

522. Great satisfaction does not come from doing what

you know you can do.

523. Sentences and paragraphs are like slug-trails of the

mind.

524. History tells us all the mistakes we are about to

make.

525. You are one quarter of a foursome when with your

parents, sister, brother, son and daughter.

526. Familiar paths are quickest to tread.

527. Cruelty stands out; it doesn't need to be sought by

suspicion.

528. Two people who agree will learn more than two

who disagree.

529. A wet dog smells worse than a dry dog.

530. Home is where the head rests easiest.

531. A mind is as deep as the depths it is willing to dive.

532. A man who stands on his principles can remain motionless forever.

533. Forgetfulness brings fretfulness; organized recollection brings calm.

534. Give children a sandwich and they will be happily nourished, give the elderly a free meal and they will demand hot plates, knives and forks, refreshments, a table and a comfortable chair.

535. The sharp witted fire warnings of their vulnerabilities.

536. The juxtaposing of words is the secret of everlasting thought.

537. No man can hang his coat in the past.

538. We carry our bones for decades before leaving

them behind.

539. In war we name our own dead and count the bodies

of enemies.

540. There is so much more to any age than the

reputation it acquires.

541. Don't argue with those who know better unless you

are prepared to be shamed.

542. The idle feign uselessness in order to fool the

helpful.

543. The detail is never as important as the flavor.

544. It is as relevant to speak of a man's skin color as it is

to speak of the color of a dog's fur; a man is a man

and a dog is a dog.

545. There can only be superiors to those who accept their inferiority.

546. Those who invest with the hope of profit should not moan if the reality is loss.

547. It is easier to create perfection than to correct imperfections in that already created.

548. We are what we are today, not what we were yesterday.

549. In others' eyes you are as wealthy as your appearance.

550. Do not judge harshly the abilities of others by the measure of your own ability.

551. Hypocrisy is a useful tool of pragmatism.

552. Great minds work not for money but for enlightenment.

553. The breadth of compassion is different in all of us.

554. Those who remember us annually are more

generous than those who forget us eternally.

555. The universe is a plethora of unfathomable light

sources.

556. Visitors have outstayed their welcome when you

leave your favorite chair.

557. Evidence is only as compelling as the reliability of

the sources from which it is collected.

558. The giver of a miserly tip receives greater disdain

than a giver of no tip.

559. All thoughts of mortality are homage to its

omnipotence.

560. The smaller earth becomes in man's perception, the

more his ambitions will point beyond it.

561. No man can empathize with a mother unless he too has experienced the practice of motherhood.

562. A mirror offers no sympathy.

563. Those who are self-reliant shall forever possess support.

564. Intelligence exposes your own ignorance.

565. Grandparents are parents without the responsibility and tension of parenthood.

566. A man loves his mother and tries to sustain his love for his wife.

567. Three carefully chosen adjective will tell us all we need to know about anyone.

568. Complex minds find solace in simplicity.

569. New love is like an unquenchable thirst.

570. A lie that is told as a lie will gain many proselytes.

571. Poor doctors are rarer than poor patients.

572. A good wife takes her husband's money but a good daughter won't take her father's.

573. Achievements are today's fetes and tomorrow's memories.

574. A nation can be judged by the success or failure of its language.

575. The loud lone voice hushes the listening masses.

576. He who acts as a leader shall become a leader.

577. Those born on the plains can travel far without obstacles.

578. Without opportunity poverty will reign supreme.

579. Our name carries with it so much more than identification.

580. Thought is the pleasurable vice of idleness.

581. No parent would hit a child if it were able to hit

back twice as hard.

582. Magic wouldn't be magical if we knew the secret of

it is performance.

583. Birthdays are milestones on an incalculable journey.

584. Money means nothing to those without wants.

585. Fitness flounders in our twenties but we realize this

years later.

586. Only hypochondriacs know when they are really ill.

587. Vast resources of experience and knowledge are

wasted when the old are pensioned off and put out

to dry.

588. Those without prospects describe life as boring.

589. Characteristics are human: how we display them is

individual.

590. An individual prioritizes loyalty until all outstanding

beneficiaries have been served.

591. Risks are calculated acts taken in the shadow of

calculated punishments.

592. Being prepared for all eventualities is sensibility

gone mad.

593. Fine buildings are the legacy of generations who

think beyond their own age.

594. A cake too big to eat can be sliced into portions.

595. A good picture carries no clutter.

596. A single set of clothes is the master of a sensible

diet.

597. Words paint pictures that are perceived differently

by each mind that views them.

598. Those born in January are blessed with perspicacity.

599. Never climb the highest mountain first.

600. A child flourishes in a world of black and white and

faces only confusion in shades of grey.

601. When the head nods and the mouth utters no,

believe the head.

602. We stand closest to our allies in thought.

603. No eldest child looks up to its siblings.

604. Beware of the overly-clean for they attempt to

wash away the stains of existence.

605. Work for money: perspire for ambition.

606. All things must come to a full stop.

607. Prepare for a child a pathway of discovery.

ABOUT THE AUTHOR

Ken Ross was born at Barmby Moor in the East Riding of Yorkshire, 1953. He was educated at Park Grove Primary School, York, and Harehills County Secondary School, Leeds. A life-long student of all things interesting, he describes himself as a writer and a thinker. His jobs include customer service clerk, betting shop manager, accounts clerk, supermarket manager, metal analyst, school dinner supervisor, nursery assistant, teaching, professional writer and author, tree surgeon, artist, photographer and home shopping delivery driver. As a single parent he raised eight children, who themselves have multiplied and gone forth. He lives in Osmondthorpe, Leeds.

16964981R00045

Made in the USA
Charleston, SC
19 January 2013